TRENDS IN SOUTHEAST ASIA

The **ISEAS – Yusof Ishak Institute** (formerly Institute of Southeast Asian Studies) is an autonomous organization established in 1968. It is a regional centre dedicated to the study of socio-political, security, and economic trends and developments in Southeast Asia and its wider geostrategic and economic environment. The Institute's research programmes are grouped under Regional Economic Studies (RES), Regional Strategic and Political Studies (RSPS), and Regional Social and Cultural Studies (RSCS). The Institute is also home to the ASEAN Studies Centre (ASC), the Singapore APEC Study Centre and the Temasek History Research Centre (THRC).

ISEAS Publishing, an established academic press, has issued more than 2,000 books and journals. It is the largest scholarly publisher of research about Southeast Asia from within the region. ISEAS Publishing works with many other academic and trade publishers and distributors to disseminate important research and analyses from and about Southeast Asia to the rest of the world.

FINANCIAL TECHNOLOGY ADOPTION IN GREATER JAKARTA

Patterns, Constraints and Enablers

Astrid Meilasari-Sugiana, Siwage Dharma Negara and Hui Yew-Foong

ISSUE
9
2022

YUSOF ISHAK INSTITUTE

Published by: ISEAS Publishing
                  30 Heng Mui Keng Terrace
                  Singapore 119614
                  publish@iseas.edu.sg
                  http://bookshop.iseas.edu.sg

This publication is made possible with the support of Konrad-Adenauer-Stiftung.

ISEAS Library Cataloguing-in-Publication Data

Name(s): Meilasari-Sugiana, Astrid, author. | Negara, Siwage Dharma, author. | Hui, Yew-Foong, author.
Title: Financial technology adoption in Greater Jakarta : patterns, constraints and enablers / by Astrid Meilasari-Sugiana, Siwage Dharma Negara, and Hui Yew-Foong.
Description: Singapore : ISEAS-Yusof Ishak Institute, May 2022. | Series: Trends in Southeast Asia, ISSN 0219-3213 ; TRS9/22 | Includes bibliographical references.
Identifiers: ISBN 9789815011548 (soft cover) | ISBN 9789815011555 (pdf)
Subjects: LCSH: Finance, Personal—Software—Jakarta (Indonesia). | Financial services industry—Technological innovations—Jakarta (Indonesia).
Classification: LCC DS501 I59T no. 9(2022)

Typeset by Superskill Graphics Pte Ltd
Printed in Singapore by Mainland Press Pte Ltd

FOREWORD

The economic, political, strategic and cultural dynamism in Southeast Asia has gained added relevance in recent years with the spectacular rise of giant economies in East and South Asia. This has drawn greater attention to the region and to the enhanced role it now plays in international relations and global economics.

The sustained effort made by Southeast Asian nations since 1967 towards a peaceful and gradual integration of their economies has had indubitable success, and perhaps as a consequence of this, most of these countries are undergoing deep political and social changes domestically and are constructing innovative solutions to meet new international challenges. Big Power tensions continue to be played out in the neighbourhood despite the tradition of neutrality exercised by the Association of Southeast Asian Nations (ASEAN).

The **Trends in Southeast Asia** series acts as a platform for serious analyses by selected authors who are experts in their fields. It is aimed at encouraging policymakers and scholars to contemplate the diversity and dynamism of this exciting region.

THE EDITORS

Series Chairman:
    Choi Shing Kwok

Series Editor:
    Ooi Kee Beng

Editorial Committee:
    Daljit Singh
    Francis E. Hutchinson
    Norshahril Saat

Financial Technology Adoption in Greater Jakarta: Patterns, Constraints and Enablers

By Astrid Meilasari-Sugiana, Siwage Dharma Negara
and Hui Yew-Foong

EXECUTIVE SUMMARY

- This article reports the findings of an online survey conducted in November–December 2021 on Indonesians' experience and perception of fintech tools, focusing on fintech adoption in the Greater Jakarta region, which besides Jakarta, includes Bogor, Depok, Tangerang and Bekasi.
- One key finding is that, in the Greater Jakarta region, socio-economic status as measured by income is not a key determinant of fintech adoption. This is likely due to the more developed and mature ICT infrastructure in the Greater Jakarta region, which makes fintech tools readily accessible.
- However, the kinds of fintech tools that are more likely to be used—M-banking, E-wallet, Online Lending, Investment, Donations, and so on—are influenced by factors such as income, education, gender, age and occupation, suggesting that different fintech tools appeal to different groups in society according to their needs and resources.
- Psychological factors that are important in the adoption of fintech include having many choices in the needed financial services and feeling in control. While fintech users are concerned about data leaks and fraud, this does not deter them from using fintech.
- It may be anticipated that with the deepening of ICT infrastructure and public education on the safe use of fintech, fintech usage in Indonesia will continue to spread throughout the country.

Financial Technology Adoption in Greater Jakarta: Patterns, Constraints and Enablers

By Astrid Meilasari-Sugiana, Siwage Dharma Negara and Hui Yew-Foong[1]

INTRODUCTION

The COVID-19 pandemic has arguably accelerated changes in consumer behaviour, leading to more people performing economic activities online. One important change is the adoption of fintech as a preferred transaction and payment method. This trend is driven by a significant proportion of the unbanked population and the lower-income segment in urban areas. New fintech start-ups such as ShopeePay (E-wallet), Shopee Paylater (Buy Now Pay Later or BNPL) and Kredivo (Online Lending Service) and Bibit (Mutual Fund Invesment) have all introduced innovative ways to offer online financial services in Indonesia's rapidly growing digital economy.

Fintech enterprises offering E-wallet, BNPL, Online Lending, Insurance and Multifinance require approval from the Financial Services Authority of Indonesia (Otoritas Jasa Keuangan or OJK),

[1] Astrid Meilasari-Sugiana is Lecturer at Bakrie University and the School of Government and Public Policy Indonesia, and Visiting Fellow at the ISEAS – Yusof Ishak Institute, Singapore. Siwage Dharma Negara is Senior Fellow at the ISEAS – Yusof Ishak Institute, Singapore. Hui Yew-Foong is Visiting Senior Fellow at the same institute. The authors would like to thank Katadata for conducting the survey. We are grateful for excellent research assistance from Neo Hui Yun Rebecca. We thank Manggi Habir, Tham Siew Yean, Cassey Lee and Monica Wihardja for useful comments and suggestions. All errors are the authors' responsibility.

whereas fintech enterprises dealing with investments, stock/mutual funds and cryptocurrencies require approval from the Commodity Futures Trading Supervisory Agency (Badan Pengawas Perdagangan Berjangka Komoditi). In 2012 OJK replaced the previous Capital Market Supervisory Board (Bapepam LK or Badan Pengawas Pasar Modal & Lembaga Keuangan) and holds wider authority in supervising and regulating the capital market and financial institutions. Fintech enterprises undergo a two-step process to obtain permits from OJK: the first involves reporting and analysing the suitability of pursuits and business processes with current government regulations; and secondly, upon further recommendations, fintech start-ups are mandated to register the business with OJK by compiling a self-assessed risk mitigation portfolio and devising a collaboration scheme with government inspectors to avoid money laundering and to establish a consumer service centre for consumer protection. The innovations brought about by fintech start-ups show similarities to the technology and business processes within the various fintech categories in Indonesia; standardization is, however, still a work in progress. This is occurring in the area of their services, their transaction and payment methods, the timeframe involved, the quality of the fintech platforms, and the rights and responsibilities of both the industry and consumers.

Along with improved services and increased transparency, fintech is gaining momentum and changing the economic landscape in urban and peri-urban areas. This is due to its decentralized, personalized and efficient nature. We observed lower psychological barriers to enable digital literacy and spread fintech adoption among Indonesia's middle- and lower-income urban households. This trend is especially relevant to merchants, owners of Micro, Small and Medium Enterprises (MSME) and members of cooperatives who, without fintech, would not be able to expand their market base beyond their immediate social network.

Moreover, the rapid development of fintech has profound social and psychological implications for users, from decreasing cyberphobia and increasing literacy to engaging highly specialized fintech miners through the smart contract functionality within blockchain platforms such as Bitcoin and Ethereum.

2

To better understand the role fintech plays in engaging various forms of capital within a rapidly digitalized landscape, ISEAS commissioned an online survey in November–December 2021.[2] The survey sought information on respondents' experience and perception of the use of fintech. Specifically, it aims to understand fintech adoption in Greater Jakarta, focusing on the reasons for fintech adoption and the drawbacks and benefits of fintech adoption for individuals.

Although the survey was conducted nationwide, the focus of the analysis in this report is on Greater Jakarta. With more than 30 million people living there, the Greater Jakarta region, including Bogor, Depok, Tangerang and Bekasi, represents around 11 per cent of Indonesia's population and has the highest number of fintech users in the country (AFTECH 2020). Given this backdrop, this survey tries to examine fintech penetration among Greater Jakarta's different socio-economic groups and understand how fintech use alters their social and economic network for empowerment, growth and inclusion.

SAMPLING, DATA COLLECTION METHODS AND SURVEY LIMITATIONS

The online survey was conducted from 25 November to 5 December 2021, specifically targeting fintech users aged 18–70 years. It uses non-probability sampling,[3] a technique that was more conducive and practical amid the ongoing COVID-19 pandemic. We also note that since sample selection is based on the subjective judgment of the researcher, they may not accurately represent the population. Therefore, we cannot easily generalize the findings to the population. Be that as it may, since we are interested in respondents with reasonable access to fintech tools, an online survey is a suitable approach for this study. The survey questionnaire was compiled based on the need to complement and advance previous surveys on the adoption of financial technology by the Indonesian population.

---

[2] The survey was conducted by PT Katadata Indonesia.

[3] https://www.questionpro.com/blog/non-probability-sampling/

There were twenty-six questions to be answered within 10–15 minutes. The survey link was circulated through Katadata's exclusive mailing list, social media accounts, and other unique distribution channels.

There were 3,157 total valid respondents, of which around 76 per cent were from Java. For our analysis in this article, we will focus on the 1,212 respondents from Greater Jakarta. Data from the 1,197 respondents from Java but outside Greater Jakarta may be used to contextualize the data from Greater Jakarta.

Figures 1 and 2 provide snapshots of the profiles of respondents. There are more female respondents (55 per cent) than male respondents (45 per cent). The largest age group is Generation Y/Millenial (23–38 years old) (58 per cent). Forty-five per cent of respondents are senior high school graduates, and 41 per cent are university graduates. Based on the Socio-economic Status (SES), the largest SES group among the respondents are from SES C (36 per cent), followed by SES D and E (23 per cent).[4] In terms of occupation, the largest group is private employees (31 per cent), followed by housewives (17 per cent), students (15 per cent), and entrepreneurs (13 per cent). Among entrepreneurs, the largest group comes from the trade/commerce sector (74.3 per cent), followed by the tourism sector (4.4 per cent).

FINANCIAL TECHNOLOGY USE IN GREATER JAKARTA

Financial technology (Fintech) has driven social transformation beyond empowerment and inclusion, to provide access to an alternative

---

[4] SES (Socio-economic Status) is a classification to categorize individuals or households based on their economic capacity and social status. Globally, SES in general is determined by the income level as the proxy. However, in Indonesia and most developing countries where there are a lot of informal workers with irregular income, income is quite difficult to measure. Therefore, monthly expenditure is used instead as a more accurate proxy for determining the SES. In this survey, SES is classified into four groups; A (monthly expenditure >Rp6 million); B (monthly expenditure Rp4.1–6 million); C (monthly expenditure Rp2–4 million); and D–E (monthly expenditure < Rp2 million).

Figure 1: Respondent Profiles by Gender, Age and Education

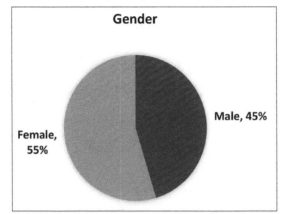

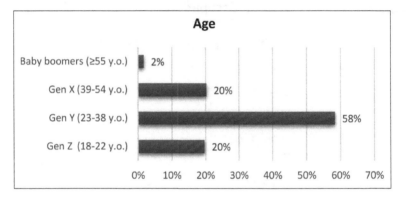

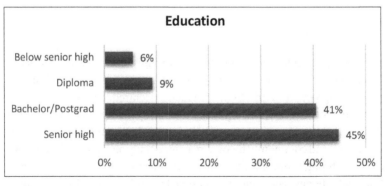

Figure 2: Respondent Profiles by Income and Occupation

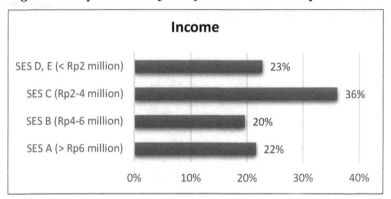

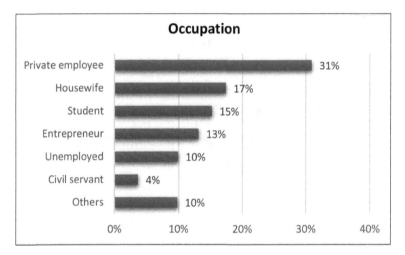

development model for communities and individuals on the periphery (Swedberg 2017). The decentralized and bottom-up nature of fintech growth signals a shift from production-centred to people-centred development. The latter incorporates social, psychological and economic deliberation for empowerment, rendering the importance of individual, household and community involvement in socially and politically relevant actions through fintech platforms (Granovetter 2017). Furthermore, financial literacy and fintech adoption by middle- and lower-income communities pave the way for a more resilient economic development as it provides financial access to a broader segment of society. The power of fintech lies in the participatory mode of decision-making it offers as well as its "ease of use" and "less cumbersome administrative requirements" for performing financial transactions. Nonetheless, for consumer protection against fraud, data leaks and loan shark lenders, OJK provides integrated regulatory oversight despite ongoing discussions at the House of Representatives on the possibility of returning the oversight role to the Central Bank. OJK remains the integrated regulatory authority for more prudent and specific oversight of financial institutions, primarily conglomerates. Alternative development movements spearheaded by fintech use acknowledge the needs and established rights of citizens and households, and hence are capable of accepting the intrinsic diversity of social lives whilst removing the structural constraints on local economic development initiatives. Structural constraints include barriers to mainstream financial systems and barriers to conventional bank lending, such as identification documents, gender-based and social-based stigmas, burgeoning domestic responsibilities for women, credit history and distance to banking facilities.

Figure 3 suggests that digital wallet (E-wallet) is Indonesia's most popular fintech platform, with GoPay, OVO, ShopeePay, Dana and LinkAja being the top five most popular apps among people with monthly expenditures of less than Rp4 million.[5] The popularity of these E-wallet enterprises is driven by their collaboration with GoJek and Grab drivers, with restaurants, food stalls and MSMEs in the food and beverage sector, with merchants and retailers selling clothes, accessories and beauty lines, with minimarkets and supermarkets for payments and top-ups, and with banks for money transfers and cash withdrawals. These E-wallet

---

[5] We classify respondents with monthly spending less than Rp4 million under the category of lower social economic status. Note that the minimum wage in the Jabodetabek area is above Rp4 million.

8

Figure 3: Financial Technology Usage by Activities (Part 1)

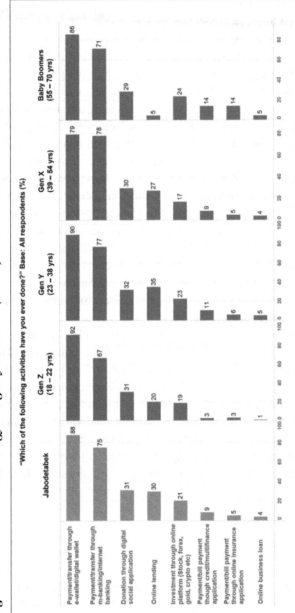

"Which of the following activities have you ever done?" Base: All respondents (%)

platforms provide customers with a "one-stop-shop" where they can find many things and even pay by scanning the QRIS code.[6]

M-banking (mobile banking) is popular due to its convenience, flexibility and confidentiality. Generations X and Y are prominent users of M-banking facilities since they are at the height of their careers, and are fairly bankable.[7] These generations are more computer literate than the baby boomers and have less resistance to transacting online. They have busy lives and have sufficient cash flow to pay for goods and services beyond subsistence, hence requiring M-banking to pay for their multifaceted needs while loving the convenience it offers. This is also why Generations X and Y are the most prominent users of online lending/online credit platforms. The four most popular online lending/online credit platforms are Akulaku, Kredivo, Julo and Indodana. They are popular since they offer small loans/credit from Rp5 million to Rp30 million, with no collateral, quick assessments and approvals, and competitive interest rates. Fintech start-ups are required by the oversight agency OJK to have a minimum capital of Rp2.5 billion, while the limit for the small loans/credit is Rp2 billion per loan, with most offering lending rates that are higher than banks (Habir 2021).

Private corporations have started using fintech to stimulate donations and raise funds through their Corporate Social Responsibility (CSR) units. Millennials (Generations Y and Z) are the most prominent users of fintech when donating. This is due to their wide-ranging and deep involvement with digital technology in their daily lives.

Since 2017, digital donations have increased by 200 per cent, with big donation organizations such as Dompet Dhuafa, Lazismu, Baznas and Laz benefiting and millennials donating an average of Rp35,000 per person per donation (Annur 2019). The Indonesian Ulema Council

---

[6] QRIS (Quick Response Indonesian Standard) code is a standardized QR code as regulated by Bank Indonesia (BI) and Asosiasi Sistem Pembayaran Indonesia (ASPI) to facilitate cashless payment in Indonesia.

[7] The term "bankable" is defined as access to a financial system in the form of payment and savings services. See Beck and De la Torre (2006).

stipulated that fintech enterprises cannot take more than one-eighth of the donated amount per person per donation. It is important that future potential niche markets such as the Shariah segment closely adhere to such stipulations.

Figure 3 shows that Multifinance and BNPL applications are more popular among Generation Y (11 per cent) and Babyboomers (14 per cent). The interest rates for BNPL range from 1.9 per cent to 3 per cent, with Kredivo, for example, offering interest rates of 2.95 per cent per month or 0.24 per cent per day (conventional banks usually offer interest rates of 2.25 per cent per month). One of the perks of Kredivo include not having to pay interest for a one-month instalment. Baby boomers using BNPL often have multiple sources of income coming in at various times (both passive and active income, though not substantially large in amount), hence they enjoy the benefits of paying later. Generation Y, who are still in their productive age, sees the need to balance spending for their multiple needs and desires. Hence BNPL offers them a chance to purchase goods and services while keeping their account balance intact. BNPL is used for buying furniture, household appliances, jewellery and household capital, such as machineries for those who own a small business.

Users of online investment platforms include university undergraduate and postgraduate students, academicians, working professionals, office employees and investment and IT experts. In Indonesia, IT experts dominate the use of blockchains, whereas users of stock, forex and gold investment platforms are mixed in terms of career backgrounds, albeit most of them come from the middle and upper-middle socio-economic groups. Fintech also plays an important role in driving alternative development processes by empowering individual household members within middle- and lower-income communities. In particular, career women, women MSME owners, women-headed households and wives who have started a business or wish to start a business noted that going digital (e.g., using e-commerce and fintech such as QRIS and digital wallet) had made them feel "having increased knowledge and skills" and "more modern and more in tune with changing technology and consumer demands" (UNICEF et al. 2021).

Figure 4 also shows that the need to feel "in control" is larger for those with an income of Rp4 million to Rp6 million and above Rp6 million

Figure 4: Emotions when Using Fintech

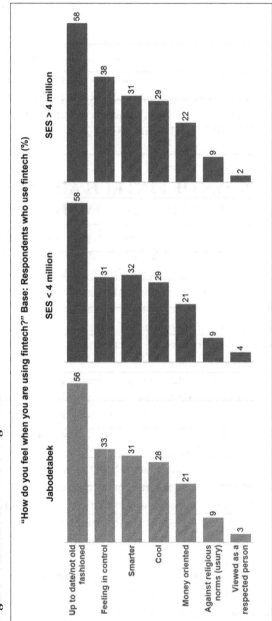

"How do you feel when you are using fintech?" Base: Respondents who use fintech (%)

(38 per cent), compared to those with a lower income of Rp2 million to Rp4 million (31 per cent). This may be because fintech users from higher income brackets feel the need to be more digitally literate throughout the whole process of engaging with fintech platforms. Also, many of the respondents with an income of Rp2 million to Rp4 million are university students, for whom fintech use enhances their feeling of being "smart", "cool" and "up to date". University students use fintech platforms in the forms of E-wallet, BNPL and online stock investments in their spare time to earn extra income (AFTECH 2020).

CATEGORIES OF FINTECH ADOPTED BY GREATER JAKARTA'S COMMUNITIES

Our survey shows that occupation, social background, economic standing and age all have an impact on the financial technology adopted by groups and individuals. Group needs, interests and stakes influence behaviour and decision-making, hence fintech penetration is contingent on their sense-making and social constructions. Moreover, the informal economic activities of Greater Jakarta's middle- and lower-income groups require the intersection of space between civil society, the corporate economy, the state and the political community. The current driver of Greater Jakarta's informal economy derives from the consumption of its middle class, especially the consumption of the Generation Y middle class. While usage among Baby Boomers has not been as high as among Generation Y users, the pandemic has raised Baby Boomers' digital literacy.

Figure 5 suggests that Generation Y is the primary user and driver of fintech platforms across the various categories, with Generation X trailing just behind. Compared to Generation Z, Generations X and Y have had a longer working life (and presumably higher salary) and better credit history. Figure 5 also suggests a notable "gap" between Generation X and Generation Y regarding fintech adoption, and this gap is even more marked between Baby Boomers and Generation Y. The latter is the generation that avidly follows the development of digital and financial technology, experimenting with and adopting the various mix

Figure 5: Financial Technology Usage by Activities (Part 2)

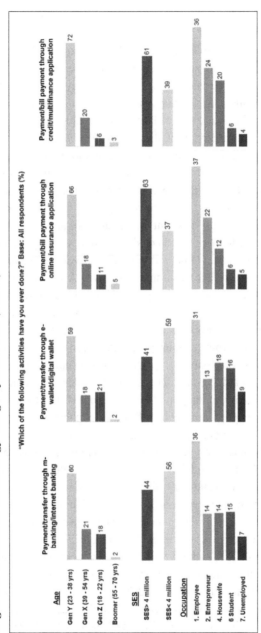

"Which of the following activities have you ever done?" Base: All respondents (%)

of fintech and digital platforms to aid, maximize and keep track of their financial standing and lifestyle.

The popularity of M-banking, E-wallet, online lending and social application/donation application for lower-income groups is depicted in Figures 5 and 6. Making purchases and buying occasional take-outs through E-wallets, performing donations through social applications and using M-banking, are still relatively affordable for them. They desire to emulate the lifestyles of the higher-income groups and experience the feelings that come with using fintech and digital platforms. Online lending tends to be dominated by lower-income groups since most are "unbanked". Those that are unbanked are insecure with face-to-face interactions in banks, cooperatives and other conventional financial institutions, and doubtful about filling out forms and answering questions. While most of the unbanked consider themselves unbankable, there is a portion that is bankable but still consider themselves unbankable.

Concerning online insurance payment, AXA is the most widely used in Greater Jakarta and beyond. This is because AXA offers wide-ranging products such as life insurance, medical coverage, chronic disease coverage, property protection, retirement funds and education savings. Apart from various products, it can be claimed online, and AXA has a strong partnership with Bank Mandiri, one of the biggest state-owned banks in Indonesia. Akulaku, Kredivo and Julo are the top three online lending platforms popularly used by lower-income groups. Their popularity comes from their extensive online and offline marketing campaigns, quick assessment and disbursement process, and adaptive payback period. They disburse credit up to Rp25–30 million. Akulaku, Kredivo, and Julo are also BNPL enterprises with attractive features such as instalment discounts, cashback and the absence of a down payment. However, one downside is that fintech customers do not usually check whether the fintech company they are borrowing from is OJK-licensed or not, and those that have difficulty paying back may, in some cases, get subjected to harsh treatment by collectors. Another problem is the tendency of overborrowing by customers, which might lead to unsustainable household debts.

The popularity of online insurance, multi-finance, and business loans among higher-income groups (Figures 5 and 6) stems from rising demand

Figure 6: Financial Technology Usage by Activities (Part 3)

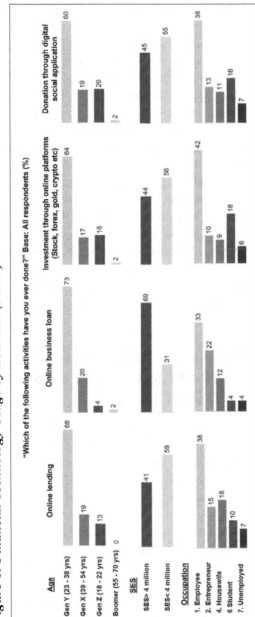

for small-scale business loans and vehicle, furniture, and household appliance instalments. This group can afford the above luxuries, and paying through online applications provides them with ease, convenience and an "easy to track system". Figure 6 shows that employees (33 per cent) take out more online business loans than entrepreneurs (22.4 per cent) because employees usually operate small side-businesses requiring small business loans available through fintech enterprises. In contrast, entrepreneurs take out much more substantial loan amounts which are solely available through the conventional banks and their relatively more rigorous assessment and screening procedures. Employees dominate the use of fintech in all categories, given their increasing consumption patterns. Peer and collegial influence substantially drive their fintech use. Compared to students, housewives and freelancers, employees have a steady flow of income. Hence they have liquid cash and/or savings available for additional spending, leading to the increased use of fintech. Moreover, employees consider themselves more financially secured; hence they are more likely to consume more, be less risk-averse, and increasingly adopt fintech than students, housewives, freelancers, and the unemployed.

FINTECH ENTERPRISES POPULAR AMONG GREATER JAKARTA'S LOWER-INCOME COMMUNITY

The adoption and continued use of fintech by MSMEs and the lower-income community require people-intensive methods of socialization, mentoring and persuasion, which appeal to their personal needs, lifestyle, identity, imagination and sense of (in)security. Also, face-to-face interactions and flexible management of investment-lending schemes are necessary when fostering fintech adoption among MSMEs and the lower-income community. Relatively better equipped with digital literacy and cultural capital, Indonesia's middle and upper-middle class have come to know and familiarize themselves with fintech through the media and their professional/collegiate circle. Appropriate financial technology platforms available through apps on cellular phones and tablets, often as an extension of existing practice, are important for adoption. Furthermore, there is the need to adapt to local conditions. An example is Shopee E-Commerce and Shopee BNPL enterprises which insert a help desk/customer service onto their platforms to reach out to and assist business start-ups. These platforms can monitor the business profile, business cycle and business cash flow of start-ups, ensuring their sustainability while fine-tuning their products and services to changing needs and circumstances.

Figure 7 shows that GoPay, Ovo, Dana, ShopeePay and Linkaja are more popular E-wallets among lower-income groups, whereas Figure 8 shows that Doku, Sakuku and Jenius are more popular among higher-income groups. This is likely because GoPay, Ovo, Dana, ShopePay and Linkaja have been around longer, advertised more online and have had more exposure among the middle- and lower-income groups compared to Doku, Sakuku and Jenius. Thus, the former group of E-wallets is more likely to come to mind first for lower and middle-income groups, and the simplicity, ease and "conciseness" of those applications make them popular among housewives. Doku, Sakuku Plus and Jenius offer additional features and services such as investments, digital banking, ATM withdrawals and debit purchases, and their offline and online marketing campaigns are targeted at higher-income groups, and therefore appeal more to those who are financially and digitally more privileged.

Figure 9 reflects the popularity of M-banking and E-wallet among men and women in Greater Jakarta. Women tend to use E-wallets more than men since women tend to take care of domestic affairs and purchase food, groceries and toiletries much more often than men do, and these are acquired through E-wallet purchases.

Other fintech services, such as online lending, investment, and donation applications, are still relatively less popular compared to E-wallet use in the Greater Jakarta area. Fintech service's popularity varies between women and men. What is interesting is that male respondents tend to use investment apps more, compared to their female counterparts (Figure 10). Meanwhile, female respondents tend to use lending and donation apps more compared to their male counterparts. For non-working women, investments are less of a matter of concern for them with their household budget. In addition, there is also a difference in fintech use between working and non-working women: working

Figure 7: E-wallet/Digital Wallet Services (Part 1)

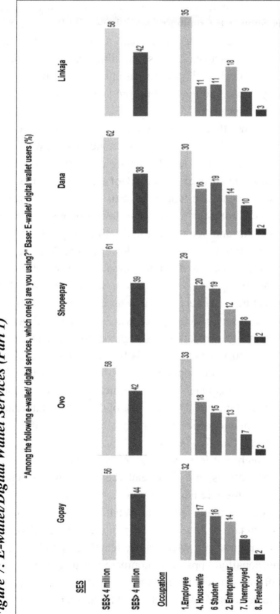

"Among the following e-wallet/ digital services, which one(s) are you using?" Base: E-wallet/ digital wallet users (%)

Figure 8: E-wallet/Digital Wallet Services (Part 2)

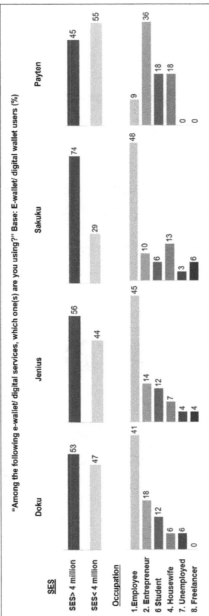

"Among the following e-wallet/ digital services, which one(s) are you using?" Base: E-wallet/ digital wallet users (%)

Figure 9: Use of M-banking and E-wallet Applications

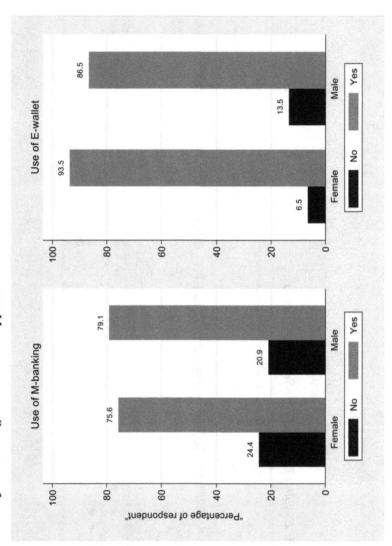

Figure 10: Use of Different Fintech Applications

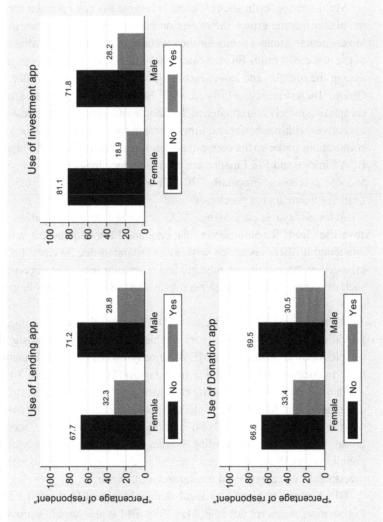

women tend to use M-banking more since M-banking is directly related to conventional banks, through which working women receive their salary.

Multi-finance applications (Figure 11) are mainly more popular among the higher income group, the exception being Adira, which caters to the lower-income group's needs for the purchase of motorcycles. Adira, one of the first credit/multi-finance enterprises established in 1991, is popular among the middle- and lower-income groups, ranking second after FIF Group. BCA Finance, affiliated with BCA Bank, has target groups comprising mostly entrepreneurs, the middle and upper-middle class and executives within urban areas. Employees, professionals, enterprises and corporations make up the core categories of consumers for BCA Finance. BCA Finance and FIF Finance are used to finance loans for motorcycles and car purchases, especially. BCA Finance appears to offer the best deals for financing car purchases.

Astra Sedaya is part of the ACC or Astra Credit Companies and advertises itself for automobile financing and heavy-equipment vehicle financing. It offers insurance services and maintenance services that are included in the instalment scheme, and is popular among entrepreneurs such as contractors and developers, as well as the middle class in urban areas.

Adira Dinamika Multi Finance (ADMF) is a multi-finance company providing largely automotive (cars and motorcycles) loans to mostly the middle to lower segment. ADMF is majority-owned by Bank Danamon (now majority-owned by MUFG from Japan) (Putri and Wareza 2019). Adira offers loans for purchasing cars, motorcycles, furniture, electronic equipment and household appliances, and hence is popular among women (especially housewives) as well as the upper-lower income group. Adira also provides online Syariah services, targeting the Muslim population, and has been diversifying its products and services to include investments, entrepreneurial capital and multi-finance.

BFI Finance is owned by local shareholders and Hanover Leasing Corporation, and went public in May 1990. BFI is also largely a provider of financing for cars and motorcycles, specializing in second-hand or used four- and two-wheelers. Adira, in contrast, largely focuses on new cars and motorcycles. BFI Finance is chosen by entrepreneurs and those

Figure 11: Credit/Multi-finance Application Services

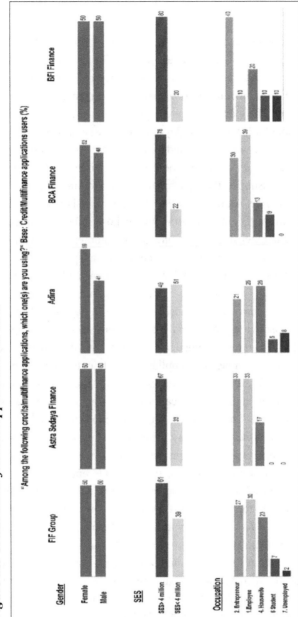

"Among the following credits/multifinance applications, which one(s) are you using?" Base: Credit/Multifinance applications users (%)

in higher-income groups. BFI specializes in credit disbursement for investments, for MSME business start-ups and for purchasing capital and productive assets such as machinery and heavy equipment. It is clear that entrepreneurs are the main target group for BFI Finance.

Where Online Lending Services are concerned, Akulaku and Kredivo are popular due to their strong marketing campaigns, whereas GoPay Paylater and Shopee Paylater are popular due to their affiliations with the already popular E-wallets GoPay and ShopeePay, which collaborate with numerous merchants, food and beverage outlets and delivery drivers (Figure 12). GoPay and ShopeePay have direct links to the GoPay Paylater and Shopee Paylater applications, facilitating easy access and one-stop service. Akulaku, GoPay Paylater and Shopee Paylater are the top three online lending platforms among those in the lower-income group due to their extensive online and offline marketing campaigns, quick assessment and disbursement process, and adaptive payback period. They disburse credits up to Rp30 million. Akulaku, GoPay Paylater and Shopee Paylater also have attractive features such as instalments, discounts, cashback and the absence of a down payment. The popularity of online insurance, BNPL and business loans among the upper-income group stems from their rising demand for insurance, small-scale business loans and vehicle/household appliance instalments. These upper-income groups can afford the above luxuries and enjoy the ease and convenience of paying through online applications while tracking their orders.

The Mutual Fund Investment application most widely used in Indonesia is Bibit (Figure 13). Bibit and Ajaib are quite popular due to their marketing campaigns, accessibility and popularity among employees, university students, professionals and retail and first-time investors. Bibit thus functions as a marketplace for various mutual fund investment platforms managed by diverse investment managers, and caters for low-risk, money-market investments, high-risk, corporate-stock investments, fixed-return investments, and mixed investments.

Other mutual fund investment applications, such as Koinworks and Amartha, are also available (Figure 14). Koinworks services more urban populations, while Amartha services more rural and peri-urban areas. The majority of their clients are MSMEs.

Figure 12: Online Lending Services

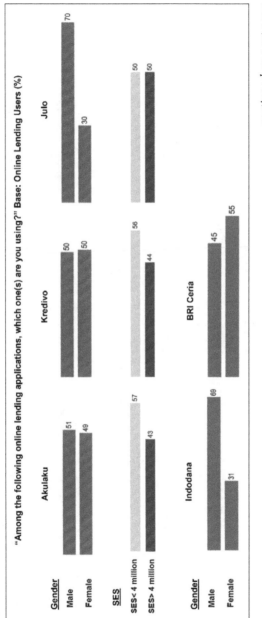

"Among the following online lending applications, which one(s) are you using?" Base: Online Lending Users (%)

continued on next page

25

Figure 12 — continued

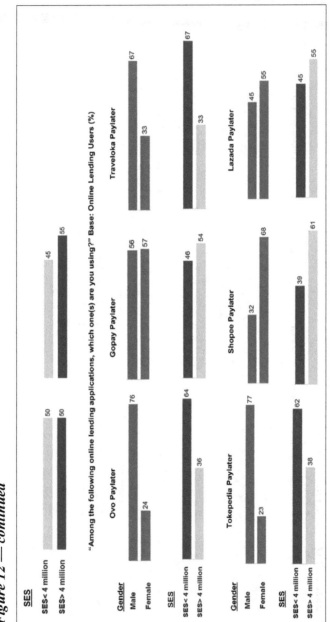

"Among the following online lending applications, which one(s) are you using?" Base: Online Lending Users (%)

Figure 13: Mutual Fund Investment Services (Part 1)

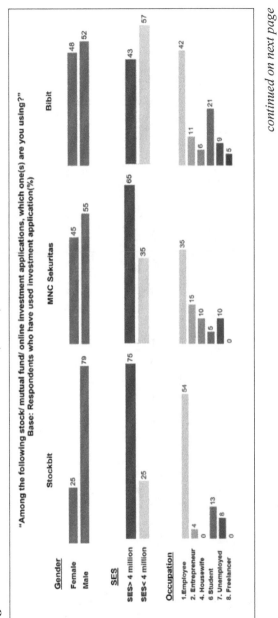

"Among the following stock/ mutual fund/ online investment applications, which one(s) are you using?"
Base: Respondents who have used investment application(%)

continued on next page

Figure 13 — continued

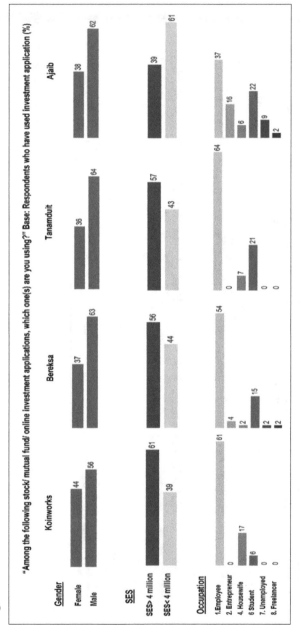

"Among the following stock/ mutual fund/ online investment applications, which one(s) are you using?" Base: Respondents who have used investment application (%)

Figure 14: Mutual Fund Investment Services (Part 2)

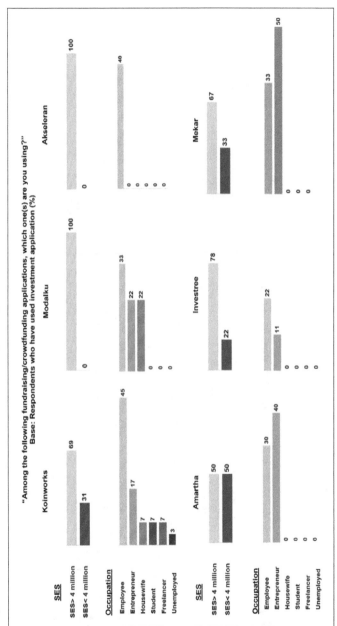

"Among the following fundraising/crowdfunding applications, which one(s) are you using?"
Base: Respondents who have used investment application (%)

Figure 15: Obstacles to Using Financial Technology (Part 1)

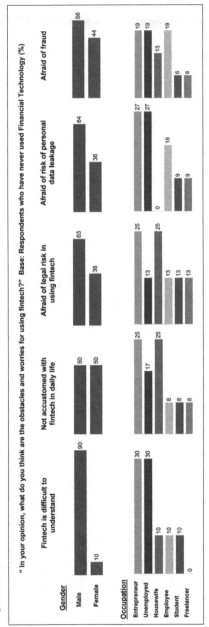

" In your opinion, what do you think are the obstacles and worries for using fintech?" Base: Respondents who have never used Financial Technology (%)

Figure 16: Obstacles to Using Financial Technology (Part 2)

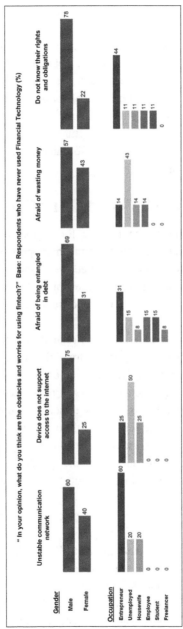

" In your opinion, what do you think are the obstacles and worries for using fintech?" Base: Respondents who have never used Financial Technology (%)

Finally, fintech applications appear to be more prevalent in Greater Jakarta than in other provinces. This may be because of greater ICT availability and higher salary/income in Greater Jakarta compared to other provinces (Databoks n.d.). The abundance, speed and density of information flow in the Greater Jakarta area also influence decisions to donate online and speed up the collection and disbursement process while helping to ensure the transparency and accountability of donation organizations. Better ICT infrastructure makes fintech services more readily available, accessible and affordable for populations within the Greater Jakarta area.

CONSTRAINTS FOR FINTECH ADOPTION

Networking is one of the reasons for digital and fintech adoption. Users see the correlation between fintech adoption and the multi-lateral opportunities they engender. Nonetheless, their adoption of fintech and digital technology, as well as their bulk of informal work, remains essential for the objective of subsistence rather than capital accumulation (Friedman 1992).

Emerging issues and contentions related to fintech use include fake E-Commerce accounts/businesses, fraudulence in E-wallet payments, fraudulent goods and services, and extortion in instalment payments by unauthorized online lenders. Survey respondents in Figure 15 and Figure 16 noted that the six primary factors impeding the use of fintech include "afraid of fraud/scams", "afraid of the risk of personal data leaks", "afraid will be wasteful in spending money" or "afraid that it will lead to 'addiction' to uncontrollable spending", "unstable network", "afraid will be entangled in debt" and "afraid of legal risks involving fintech".

Respondents are more afraid of data leaks than fraud (Figure 17). This shows that respondents are quite digitally literate, have quite good access to information, and are linked to ICT social networks. Moreover, since fintech users and ICT professionals are greater in number within the Greater Jakarta area than in other regions, crimes involving fintech are much more likely to be noticed by those in the Greater Jakarta area. Fear of fraud and data leaks do not deter enthusiasm in experimenting with

Figure 17: Obstacles to Using Financial Technology

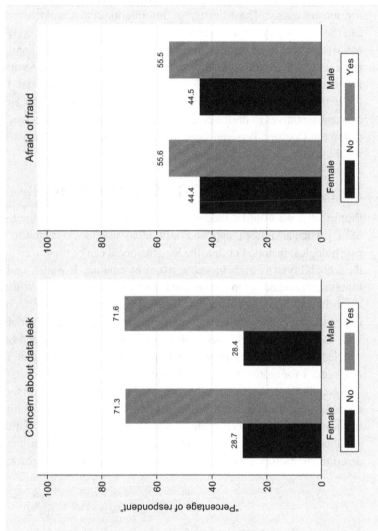

fintech. Nonetheless, there is the need to feel more secure and digitally literate when using fintech. Hence, government roles for mainstreaming and mentoring vulnerable groups for safe, adaptive and enabling fintech use are necessary. The Ministry of Information and Communications and the Ministry of MSMEs currently work with community groups and MSME owners to educate them on the benefits and potential liabilities associated with fintech use. Minister of Communications and Informatics Regulation No. 20 of 2016 (Regulation 20/2016) on Personal Data Protection on Electronic System is currently being used by the House of Representatives to draft new legislation for consumer data protection called the Codified Personal Data Protection Law (PDPL Draft) which will be enacted as law in the near term.[8]

ENABLERS FOR FINTECH ADOPTION

Empirically, we want to understand the relationship between the usage of a particular fintech app and individual user socioeconomic and psychological factors. For this, the logistic model can be used to estimate the probability of a certain fintech app (i.e., M-banking, E-wallet, lending, investment, and donation app) being used by the respondent. The model controls individual-specific characteristics, such as age, gender, income, job type, and residential area. It also includes psychological variables, such as feeling in control, being afraid of data leaks or fraud, and being worried about being extravagant or trapped in unsustainable debt. (See Appendix 1 for more detailed estimation procedures.)

Overall, the estimation results show that having many choices for the needed financial services and feeling in control increase the probability of an individual using fintech applications. These variables are statistically significant and positive in all model estimations. Table 1 summarizes the determining factors underlying individual preference to use particular

---

[8] More analysis on fintech regulations in Indonesia, the institutions responsible for supervising fintech enterprises and the fintech licensing processes will be covered in a forthcoming *ISEAS Perspective*.

Table 1: *Determining Factors for Fintech Use in Greater Jakarta*

M-banking	E-wallet	Lending	Investment	Donation
Higher education	Woman	Woman	Man	Woman
Has a permanent/full-time work	Younger people	Worried about data leaks	Younger people	Higher education
Worried about data leaks	Those who want more financial control (in control)	Feeling that you have many choices for the financial services you need	Higher education	Those who want more financial control (in control)
Feeling that you have many choices for the financial services you need	Worried about data leaks	Worried about being trapped in debt	Has a permanent/full-time work	Worried about data leaks
Feel that lifestyle changes are becoming more wasteful	Feeling that you have many choices for the financial services you need	Feel easier to get capital	Those who want more financial control (in control)	Feeling that you have many choices for the financial services you need
			Worried about data leaks	Use fintech for social activities
			Feeling that you have many choices for the financial services you need	Use fintech for broadening network
			Feel easier to get capital	
			Use fintech for social activities	

fintech applications. For instance, those who have higher education (university graduate) and have a full-time job have a higher probability of using M-banking since they are part of the banked population, by virtue of education and, therefore their occupational grouping. Young women have a higher probability of using E-wallets, while young and higher educated men prefer to use investment apps. Higher educated women also have a higher probability of using donation apps.

Social and economic stratification influence fintech inclusion among Indonesia's medium-and low-income communities, with fintech being most accessible and widely used among small- and medium-scale producers/traders who capitalize on their personal goods for profit and are embedded within both the value chain and production chain network. Fintech is also widely accessible and adopted among professionals, private and public sector employees, university students, academicians, wholesalers and retailers (through platforms such as E-Commerce, E-wallet, Online/P2P Lending, Insurance, BNPL, Credit/Multi-Financing and Investments). Fintech is somewhat accessible and somewhat adopted among micro home industries, women-headed MSMEs and women-headed households of the lower- and low-middle income brackets; this is probably due to the tendency for women to experience cyberphobia when using digital platforms and digital technology. Blue-collar men who are embedded in the production chain and own capital have a much higher propensity for adopting fintech (e.g., GoJek drivers who pay instalments for their vehicles) compared to their pink-collar women counterparts in the same social strata (e.g., women sweatshop/textile workers who are also cosmetics, clothing and accessories resellers/retailers). MSMEs in urban areas are much more likely to adopt fintech than those in rural areas, whereas agricultural commodity traders and farmers are much less likely to adopt E-Commerce and fintech compared to MSMEs in rural areas.

Survey results in Figure 18 and Figure 19 suggest that the top three motivating factors for fintech adoption are easy access to financial services and business financing, convenience/accessibility, and accelerating business for income generation. This finding is not surprising given that the top four groups of survey respondents are private employees, MSME owners/entrepreneurs, students and housewives.

Figure 18: Motivation for Using Financial Technology (Part 1)

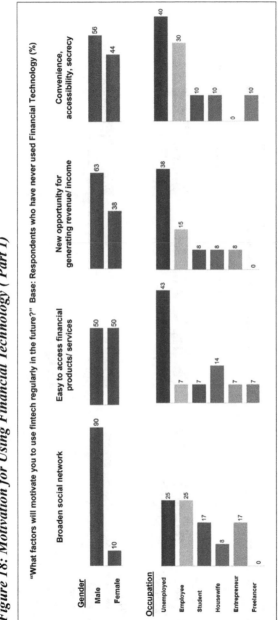

"What factors will motivate you to use fintech regularly in the future?" Base: Respondents who have never used Financial Technology (%)

Figure 19: Motivation for Using Financial Technology (Part 2)

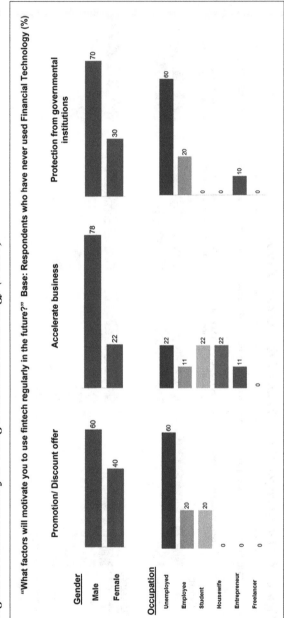

"What factors will motivate you to use fintech regularly in the future?"   Base: Respondents who have never used Financial Technology (%)

Fintech use for lifestyle and consumption purposes provides users with identity recognition, validation and differentiation. This type of fintech user usually has one to two E-wallets, uses one to two E-Commerce platforms for making purchases, and is affiliated with one BNPL or online credit enterprise. In general, data leaks and fraud do not deter interest in fintech adoption, and the momentum for the use of E-wallet, Mobile Banking, BNPL and Multi-Finance is still growing at a steady rate, and investment platforms are slowly gaining trust from employees outside the professional circle.

The hallmark of social and economic empowerment includes living beyond subsistence, participating beyond consumption, and striving towards capital accumulation, investments and business development. Government protection measures for MSMEs and for businesses from the lower-income group incorporated into the supply chain network and the digital economy (through mainstreaming, government aid/subsidy and tax refund) are essential for their empowerment. Digital and fintech platforms are one of the drivers for transforming groups and communities from the former to the latter, hence fostering upward social and economic mobility. The move from subsistence and consumption to capital accumulation and production by way of digital and fintech platforms is incremental and influenced by external push factors as opposed to internal pull factors. The need for fintech for personal branding, capital acquisition and efficient production comes at a later stage after having experimented with fintech and the digital economy for some period of time. Nonetheless, household debt can become a problem with the proliferation of fintech enterprises, given the difficulty of assessing the household finances of potential fintech users.

Typically, the average user adopts fintech due to the increasing options for desired financial services and their convenience (Figure 20). Fintech adoption is only indirectly linked to financial and entrepreneurial capital acquisition. Convenience, range of choice, financial and digital literacy, networks and formal/informal support systems all play intermediary roles in fintech adoption. The correlation between motivation for adopting fintech and awareness for network expansion through fintech is indirect. Nonetheless, MSME owners are very cognizant of the impact that digital and fintech adoption can have on business expansion.

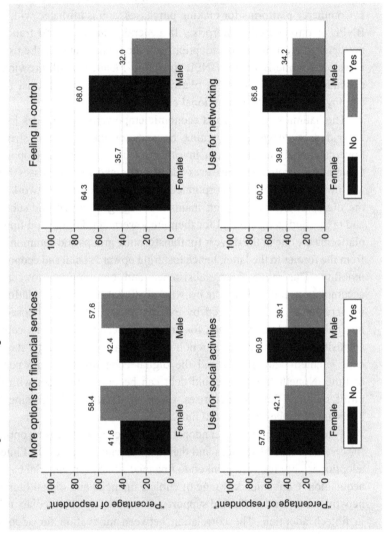

Figure 20: Motivation for Fintech Adoption

CONCLUSION

Social and economic stratification influences fintech adoption and the motivations behind them. In general, this study suggests the popularity of Mobile Banking/Online Payment, E-wallet, Multi-Finance/Credit and Buy Now Pay Later platforms over Investment, Donation and Online Business Loan platforms. It also suggests that having many choices for the needed financial services and feeling in control of their economic activities encourages people to use various fintech applications. Unsurprisingly, preferences vary across demographic and socioeconomic groups. For instance, men are more likely to use investment apps, while women are more likely to use E-wallet and lending apps. Generations Y and Z are more likely to use E-wallet and investment apps than the older generation (Generation X). Those with higher education (post senior high school) are also more likely to use fintech, especially M-banking, investment apps and donation apps, compared to those with lower education. And people who have full-time jobs are more likely to use M-banking and investment apps than those without full-time jobs. Finally, lower-income groups are more likely to use E-wallet apps, while the higher income groups are more likely to use M-banking apps. In short, the propensity to use fintech apps and the types of fintech apps used depends on one's position in society, and our study shows that this is determined not simply by socioeconomic status as measured by income, but by other factors such as age and education as well.

Our study indicates that fintech use is not directly associated with expanding the social web. That means that people do not initially think of fintech as a means to broaden their network. However, those who use fintech for social activities tend to install E-wallet, donation and investment apps.

While all fintech users are worried about data leaks and fraud, there are positive and statistically significant associations between these concerns with fintech use. One possible reason for this is that worries about data leaks do not stop people from using fintech, but instead make them more careful and well-informed. In other words, while it may not be straightforward that fintech is socially empowering, respondents have continued to use fintech tools and they are not ignorant of the potential dangers involved. Perhaps this is due to the more extensive and mature ICT infrastructure and more prevalent use of ICT in the Greater Jakarta Area, which suggests fintech adoption in Indonesia will grow in tandem with the development of ICT infrastructure throughout the country.

APPENDIX: A LOGISTIC MODEL FOR FINTECH ADOPTION

This section analyses the relationship between the usage of a particular fintech app and individual user socioeconomic and psychological factors. We use logistic regression to empirically verify the factors affecting personal decisions to use fintech. Table A1 shows a list of dichotomous dependent variables used in the model. Y1–Y5 are dependent variables concerning usage of different fintech platforms, i.e., M-banking, E-wallet, lending, investment, and donation. Y6–Y7 are dependent variables concerning fintech usage for social activities and expanding one's network. Finally, Y8–Y9 are dependent variables concerning one's perception of data security and fraud related to fintech usage.

Table A2 shows a list of independent variables used in the estimation. It covers individual-specific characteristics such as age, gender, income, job type, and residential area. It also covers some psychological factors, such as feeling in control, being afraid of data leaks or fraud, and being worried about being extravagant or trapped in unsustainable debt, among others.

Overall, the estimation results show that having many choices for the needed financial services (KAT_CHOICE) and feeling in control (KAT_TAKE_CONTROL) make people like to use various types of fintech applications. These variables are statistically significant and positive in all model estimations (Table A3).

Table A3 shows that men tend to like investment apps, while women tend to like E-wallet and lending apps (KAT_GENDER). Younger people (Generations Y and Z) tend to like E-wallet and investment apps (KAT_AGE). Those with higher education (post senior high school) tend to use fintech more, especially M-banking, investment apps and donation apps (KAT_EDUC), compared to those with lower education. And people who have full-time jobs tend to like fintech, i.e., M-banking and investment apps (KAT_JOB). Finally, lower-income groups tend to like E-wallet apps (KAT_SES), while the higher income groups tend to like M-banking apps.

Location variable (KAT_AREA) stands out as significant in all estimations (Table A3). It shows that those living in the Jabodetabek area

Table A1: Dependent Variables

No.	Variable	Category	Note
Y1	KAT_MBANKING	Using M-banking = 1 Not using M-banking = 0	Most popular M-banking apps: BCA, Mandiri, BNI and BRI
Y2	KAT_EWALLET	Using E-wallet = 1 Not using E-wallet = 0	Most popular E-wallet apps: Gopay, Ovo, Shopeepay, and Dana
Y3	KAT_LENDING	Using lending app = 1 Not using lending app = 0	Most popular apps: Akulaku, Kredivo, Shopeepaylater, and Gopaylater
Y4	KAT_INVEST	Using investment app = 1 Not using investment app = 0	Most popular apps: Koinworks, Amartha, Ajaib and Bibit
Y5	KAT_DONATION	Using donation app = 1 Not using donation app = 0	Most popular apps: Kitabisa and Rumahzakat
Y6	KAT_SOCIAL_ACT	Using fintech for social activities = 1 otherwise = 0	Use as control variable for fintech app usage
Y7	KAT_BROADEN_NET	Using fintech for broadening network = 1 otherwise = 0	Use as control variable for fintech app usage
Y8	KAT_DATA_LEAK	Worried about data leak = 1 otherwise = 0	Use as control variable for fintech app usage
Y9	KAT_FRAUD	Worried about fraud = 1 otherwise = 0	Use as control variable for fintech app usage

Table A2: Control Variables

No.	Variable	Category
1	AGE	Continuous: 18–68
2	GENDER	Male = 1, Female = 0
3	KAT_AREA	Jabodetabek = 1, outside Jabodetabek = 0
4	KAT_SES	Lower middle income = 1, upper middle income = 0
5	KAT_EDUC	Senior High and below =1, higher education = 0
6	KAT_JOB	Part-time worker, unemployed = 1, full-time worker =0
7	KAT_RELATION_USE	Friends and family influence = 1, without friends and family influence = 0
8	KAT_TAKE_CONTROL	Feel in control = 1, otherwise = 0
9	KAT_DATA_LEAK	Worried about data leak = 1, otherwise = 0
10	KAT_FRAUD	Worried about fraud = 1, otherwise = 0
11	KAT_CHOICE	Feeling to have many choices for the financial services = 1, otherwise = 0
12	KAT_XTRAVAGANT	Feel becoming more wasteful = 1, otherwise = 0=
13	KAT_EASY_USE	Feel the ease of doing various activities = 1, otherwise = 0
14	KAT_IN_DEBT	Worried about being in unsustainable debt = 1, otherwise = 0
15	KAT_BUSINESS	Feel easy to get capital = 1, otherwise = 0
16	KAT_SOCIAL_ACT	Using fintech for social activities = 1, otherwise = 0
17	KAT_BROADEN_NET	Using fintech for broadening network = 1, otherwise = 0

Table A3: Estimation Results—Odds Ratio (Full sample)

Use of	(1) M-banking	(2) E-wallet	(3) Lending	(4) Investment	(5) Donation
gender	0.994	0.555***	0.700***	1.679***	0.807*
	(−0.07)	(−5.11)	(−3.68)	(4.87)	(−1.99)
age	1.014**	0.964***	0.998	0.980**	0.985*
	(2.66)	(−6.03)	(−0.28)	(−3.11)	(−2.40)
kat_area	1.754***	1.904***	1.811***	1.308*	1.735***
	(6.14)	(5.11)	(6.13)	(2.51)	(5.15)
kat_educ	0.399***	1.076	0.874	0.465***	0.447***
	(−9.29)	(0.59)	(−1.30)	(−6.72)	(−7.03)
kat_job	0.558***	1.213	0.971	0.570***	0.777
	(−5.40)	(1.31)	(−0.23)	(−3.55)	(−1.64)
kat_ses	0.733***	1.251*	1.048	0.910	0.847
	(−3.37)	(1.96)	(0.47)	(−0.86)	(−1.48)
kat_relation_use	1.385***	0.980	0.812*	0.720**	1.024
	(3.57)	(−0.17)	(−2.05)	(−2.93)	(0.21)
kat_take_control	1.181	1.959***	1.319**	1.758***	1.314*
	(1.67)	(4.56)	(2.70)	(5.20)	(2.45)
kat_data_leak	1.322**	2.353***	1.845***	1.849***	1.405*
	(2.83)	(6.77)	(5.16)	(4.61)	(2.56)

kat_fraud	1.207	1.274	0.942	0.861	1.158
	(1.92)	(1.85)	(−0.56)	(−1.28)	(1.24)
kat_choice	1.336**	1.607***	1.456***	1.748***	1.329*
	(3.24)	(4.11)	(3.66)	(4.83)	(2.49)
kat_xtravagant	1.322**	1.013	1.265*	1.151	1.232
	(2.63)	(0.09)	(2.16)	(1.16)	(1.70)
kat_in_debt	1.354*	1.244	3.726***	1.307	0.954
	(1.98)	(1.10)	(9.23)	(1.54)	(−0.25)
kat_business	1.040	0.951	2.187***	1.615***	0.925
	(0.30)	(−0.29)	(6.30)	(3.52)	(−0.53)
kat_social_act	1.294**	1.511**	1.032	2.037***	8.458***
	(2.60)	(2.99)	(0.30)	(6.58)	(19.42)
kat_broaden_network	1.069	0.822	0.833	0.814	0.661***
	(0.75)	(−1.68)	(−1.81)	(−1.85)	(−3.68)
N	2933	2933	2933	2933	2933

Notes: Exponentiated coefficients; z statistics in parentheses; $* \ p < 0.05$, $** \ p < 0.01$, $*** \ p < 0.001$.

have a higher probability of using fintech platforms than those outside Jabodetabek. Later we re-estimate the model using the Jabodetabek sample to check the robustness of the estimation results.

Table A4 indicates that fintech use is not associated with expanding social networks (KAT_BROADEN NETWORK). However, people who use fintech for social activities (KAT_SOCIAL_ACT) tend to install E-wallet, donation and investment apps. All fintech users are worried about data leaks (KAT_DATA_LEAK) and fraud (KAT_FRAUD). There are positive and statistically significant associations with fintech use. One possible reason for this is that worries about data leaks do not stop them from using fintech but instead make people more careful and well-informed. This observation requires further study.

The following section looks at the case of Jabodetabek. We re-estimate the same model specifications on the Jabodetabek dataset. We find most of the results are consistent with previous findings using the full dataset.

Similar to the previous story, the estimation results show that the feeling to have many choices for the needed financial services (KAT_CHOICE) and feeling in control (KAT_TAKE_CONTROL) encourage people to use various types of fintech applications (Table A5).

Also, men tend to like investment apps, while women tend to like E-wallet and lending apps (KAT_GENDER). Younger people tend to like E-wallet, investment and donation apps (KAT_AGE). Those with higher education (post senior high school) tend to use fintech more than those with lower education (KAT_EDUC). And people who have full-time jobs tend to like fintech, i.e., M-banking and investment apps (KAT_JOB).

What is interesting in Jabodetabek is that income (KAT_SES) is not significantly associated with the probability of fintech use. One possible explanation is that the widespread access, better ICT infrastructure, and broader network effect have provided equal access to all levels of income groups. This indicates that equal access to fintech has led to a more inclusive society in Jabodetabek.

Corroborating the previous finding (with full dataset), Table A6 shows that fintech tends not to be used to expand social networks (KAT_BROADEN NETWORK). Nevertheless, people still use fintech

Table A4: Estimation Results—Odds Ratio (Full Sample)

	(1) social_activities	(2) broaden_network	(3) data_leak	(4) concern of fraud
kat_mbanking	1.180 (1.57)	1.293** (2.91)	1.596*** (5.12)	1.555*** (4.94)
kat_ewallet	1.728*** (3.88)	1.013 (0.11)	3.091*** (9.82)	2.179*** (6.66)
kat_invest	1.560*** (3.75)	0.988 (−0.11)	1.706*** (4.26)	1.109 (0.97)
kat_lending	0.869 (−1.27)	0.905 (−1.06)	1.671*** (4.73)	1.213* (2.04)
kat_donation	8.006*** (19.04)	0.898 (−1.08)	1.585*** (3.98)	1.411*** (3.42)
gender	0.905 (−1.07)	0.973 (−0.35)	0.814* (−2.43)	0.871 (−1.73)
age	1.012* (2.26)	0.982*** (−3.98)	1.022*** (4.37)	1.005 (1.19)
kat_area	1.143 (1.41)	0.724*** (−3.96)	1.344*** (3.35)	1.352*** (3.70)
kat_educ	0.815* (−2.03)	1.082 (0.91)	0.822* (−2.06)	0.755** (−3.21)
kat_job	0.901 (−0.83)	1.088 (0.83)	0.877 (−1.21)	0.977 (−0.22)
kat_ses	1.001 (0.01)	0.964 (−0.45)	1.373*** (3.62)	1.220* (2.41)
N	2933	2933	2933	2933

Notes: Exponentiated coefficients; z statistics in parentheses; * $p < 0.05$, ** $p < 0.01$, *** $p < 0.001$.

Table A5: Estimation Results—Odds Ratio (Jabodetabek)

Use of	(1) M-banking	(2) E-wallet	(3) lending	(4) investment	(5) donation
gender	1.306 (1.72)	0.454*** (-3.58)	0.728* (-2.27)	1.961*** (4.35)	0.945 (-0.37)
age	0.994 (-0.65)	0.954*** (-4.05)	0.992 (-1.02)	0.963*** (-3.83)	0.973** (-3.07)
kat_educ	0.330*** (-6.52)	0.678 (-1.63)	0.938 (-0.43)	0.434*** (-4.89)	0.500*** (-4.20)
kat_job	0.480*** (-3.70)	1.156 (0.48)	1.131 (0.63)	0.594* (-2.15)	0.735 (-1.34)
kat_ses	0.748 (-1.77)	1.065 (0.28)	1.019 (0.13)	0.922 (-0.50)	0.947 (-0.34)
kat_relation_use	0.989 (-0.07)	0.945 (-0.24)	0.823 (-1.31)	0.764 (-1.62)	1.153 (0.89)
kat_take_control	1.221 (1.15)	2.601** (3.17)	1.199 (1.25)	1.992*** (4.40)	1.395* (2.14)
kat_data_leak	1.652** (2.86)	2.934*** (4.40)	2.055*** (3.97)	2.048*** (3.43)	1.371 (1.62)

kat_fraud	1.374	1.013	0.948	0.641**	1.174
	(1.89)	(0.05)	(−0.35)	(−2.64)	(0.97)
kat_choice	1.613**	2.867***	1.501**	1.719**	1.409*
	(2.97)	(4.51)	(2.70)	(3.15)	(2.09)
kat_xtravagant	1.713**	1.102	1.236	1.176	1.187
	(2.85)	(0.38)	(1.39)	(0.94)	(1.00)
kat_in_debt	1.165	1.331	4.281***	1.277	1.018
	(0.58)	(0.77)	(6.75)	(0.96)	(0.07)
kat_business	1.038	0.847	2.369***	1.640*	0.944
	(0.16)	(−0.50)	(4.58)	(2.35)	(−0.26)
kat_social_act	1.285	1.330	0.960	2.182***	8.727***
	(1.49)	(1.15)	(−0.29)	(4.95)	(13.89)
kat_broaden_network	0.942	0.623*	0.702*	0.584**	0.557***
	(−0.36)	(−2.02)	(−2.37)	(−3.18)	(−3.58)
N	1179	1179	1179	1179	1179

Notes: Exponentiated coefficients; z statistics in parentheses; * $p < 0.05$, ** $p < 0.01$, *** $p < 0.001$.

Table A6: Estimation Results—Odds Ratio (Jabodetabek)

	(1) social_activities	(2) broaden_network	(3) data_leak	(4) concern of fraud
kat_mbanking	1.076	1.184	2.067***	1.931***
	(0.41)	(1.07)	(4.49)	(4.29)
kat_ewallet	1.192	0.897	3.507***	1.956**
	(0.71)	(−0.51)	(5.79)	(3.17)
kat_invest	1.638**	0.742	1.634*	0.781
	(2.91)	(−1.85)	(2.51)	(−1.61)
kat_lending	0.767	0.775	1.991***	1.239
	(−1.72)	(−1.84)	(4.14)	(1.60)
kat_donation	8.465***	0.940	1.399*	1.438**
	(13.78)	(−0.43)	(1.98)	(2.59)
gender	0.840	0.847	1.057	1.064
	(−1.23)	(−1.30)	(0.39)	(0.50)
age	1.014	0.979**	1.019*	1.000
	(1.69)	(−2.90)	(2.28)	(−0.02)
kat_educ	0.838	1.621***	0.842	0.862
	(−1.17)	(3.54)	(−1.12)	(−1.11)
kat_job	0.884	0.979	0.754	0.910
	(−0.59)	(−0.12)	(−1.47)	(−0.53)
kat_ses	0.915	0.933	1.096	1.001
	(−0.61)	(−0.53)	(0.62)	(0.01)
N	1179	1179	1179	1179

Notes: Exponentiated coefficients; z statistics in parentheses; * $p < 0.05$, ** $p < 0.01$, *** $p < 0.001$.

for social activities (KAT_SOCIAL_ACT), mostly through donation and investment apps.

And confirming the previous story with the full dataset, in the Jabodetabek case, all fintech users are worried about data leaks and fraud. There are positive and statistically significant associations between concern of data security and fraud risk with fintech use.

REFERENCES

Annur, Cindy Mutia. 2019. "Donasi Digital Naik Lebih dari Dua Kali Lipat Sejak 2017". *Katadata.co.id,* 27 May 2019. https://katadata. co.id/desysetyowati/digital/5e9a518a04cd0/donasi-digital-naik-lebih-dari-dua-kali-lipat-sejak-2017 (accessed 17 February 2022).

Asosiasi Fintech Indonesia (AFTECH). 2020. *Fintech Indonesia: Annual Member Survey 2019/2020.* Jakarta: AFTECH.

Beck, T., and A. De la Torre. 2006. "The Basic Analytics of Access to Financial Services". *World Bank Policy Research Working Paper* 4026, October.

Blakely, E. 2002. *Planning Local Economic Development: Theory and Practice.* London: Sage Publications.

Databoks. N.d. "Capai Rp 274 juta, PDRB Per Kapita DKI Jakarta Tertinggi Nasional pada 2021". https://databoks.katadata.co.id/datapublish/2022/02/09/capai-rp-274-juta-pdrb-per-kapita-dki-jakarta-tertinggi-nasional-pada-2021

Friedman, J. 1992. *Empowerment: The Politics of Alternative Development.* Cambridge, Massachusetts: Blackwell Press.

Granovetter, M. 2017. *Society and Economy: Framework and Principles.* Cambridge, Massachusetts: Harvard University Press.

Habir, Manggi Taruna. 2021. "The Pandemic's Benefits for Indonesia's Fintech Sector". *ISEAS Perspective*, no. 2021/100, 28 July 2021, https://www.iseas.edu.sg/wp-content/uploads/2021/07/ISEAS_Perspective_2021_100.pdf (accessed 25 April 2022).

Putri, Cantika Adinda, and Monica Wareza. 2019. "Sah! Zurich Akuisisi 80% Saham Asuransi Adira dari Danamon". CNBC Indonesia, 28 November 2019. https://www.cnbcindonesia.com/market/20191128142951-17-118726/sah-zurich-akuisisi-80-saham-asuransi-adira-dari-danamon (accessed 14 February 2022).

Swedberg, R. 2017. *The Sociology of Economic Life.* 3rd ed. Boulder, Colorado: Westview Press.

UNICEF, UNDP, Prospera, and SMERU. 2021. *Analysis of the Social and Economic Impacts of COVID-19 on Households and Strategic Policy Recommendations for Indonesia.* Jakarta, Indonesia.